First World War
and Army of Occupation
War Diary
France, Belgium and Germany

59 DIVISION
176 Infantry Brigade
Headquarters
1 January 1916 - 29 February 1916

WO95/3020/1

The Naval & Military Press Ltd
www.nmarchive.com
Published in association with The National Archives

Published by

The Naval & Military Press Ltd

Unit 10 Ridgewood Industrial Park,

Uckfield, East Sussex,

TN22 5QE England

Tel: +44 (0) 1825 749494

www.naval-military-press.com

www.nmarchive.com

This diary has been reprinted in facsimile from the original. Any imperfections are inevitably reproduced and the quality may fall short of modern type and cartographic standards.

© Crown Copyright
Images reproduced by permission of The National Archives, London, England, 2015.

Contents

Document type	Place/Title	Date From	Date To
Heading	WO95/3020/1		
War Diary	St. Albans.	01/01/1916	31/01/1916
Heading	War Diary Of 176th Infantry Brigade From February 1st 1916 To February 29th 1916. (Volume II)		
War Diary	St. Albans.	01/02/1916	29/02/1916

WO/95/3020/1

176 Infantry Brigade
Headquarters

1916 Jan - Feb.

Army Form C. 2118.

176th INFANTRY BRIGADE.

WAR DIARY
or
INTELLIGENCE SUMMARY.

(Erase heading not required.)

Instructions regarding War Diaries and Intelligence Summaries are contained in F.S. Regs., Part II. and the Staff Manual respectively. Title pages will be prepared in manuscript.

Hour, Date, Place	Summary of Events and Information	Remarks and references to Appendices
ST. ALBANS.		
January 1st, 1916.	Strength of Brigade 2472.	
January 13th, 1916.	The 59th (North Midland) Division ceases to be directly under the Command of the G.O.C. in C. Central Force, and comes under the Command of the G.O.C. 3rd.Army. Divisional Order No. 77 dated 13.1.16.	
	Battalions of the Brigade to be increased to 350 Other Ranks. 59th (North Midland) Divisional Circular Letter No. 5369/4 A. dated 13th January, 1916. Number required to complete to new establishment for Brigade :- 1386.	
January 26th 1916.	100 Short M.L. 111 Rifles issued to each Battalion in the Brigade.	
8.15 p.m. January 26th, 1916.	Information was received from 59th (North Midland) Divisional Headquarters of Zeppelins near to the coast. Units were notified, but no report was received from Battalions of aircraft being sighted.	
6.30 p.m. January 31st, 1916.	Information received from 59th (North Midland) Divisional Headquarters of three Zeppelins on the way to London working from CAMBRIDGE, and later that two Zeppelins were at BROXBOURNE. Units were informed, and orders issued for Look-Out and Firing Parties to be posted; the latter were withdrawn at 9.30 p.m. no aircraft having been reported or notification received from Divisional Headquarters of their nearer approach.	
January 31st, 1916.	Strength of Brigade 2346.	

Confidential

War Diary

of.

176th Infantry Brigade

from February 1st 1916 to February 29th 1916.

(Volume II)

Army Form C. 2118.

176th INFANTRY BRIGADE.
WAR DIARY
or
INTELLIGENCE SUMMARY.
(Erase heading not required.)

Instructions regarding War Diaries and Intelligence Summaries are contained in F. S. Regs., Part II. and the Staff Manual respectively. Title pages will be prepared in manuscript.

Hour, Date, Place	Summary of Events and Information	Remarks and references to Appendices
ST. ALBANS.		
1..2...16.	The Venbl. Archdeacon L.Klugh proceeded to CROOKHAM for duty.	S.F.
2..2...16.	The 59th (N.M.)Division was inspected by Lieut.-General Sir A.E. Codrington, K.C.V.O., C.B. while Route Marching.	S.F.
9..2...16.	The Rev. J.Goodacre, C.F. reported for duty as Brigade Chaplain vice The Venbl. Archdeacon L. Klugh.	S.F.
14..2...16.	Major T.A.Walsh, Somerset Light Infantry reported for duty as Brigade Major vice Captain C.O.Langley, 2/6th South Staffordshire Regiment. Captain C.O.Langley assumed duty as Staff Captain vice Captain A.E.Wiley, 2/5th South Staffordshire Regiment.	S.F.
	Major-General R.N.R. Reade, C.B. having proceeded to take up another appointment, hands over the Command of the Division. Major-General A.L.Sandbach, C.B., D.S.O. having been appointed to Command the Division, takes over the Command from this date.	S.F.
15..2..16.	Colonel H.A.Chandos-Pole-Gell vacates the Command of the Brigade.	S.F.
16..2..16.	Brigadier-General L.R.Carleton, D.S.O. assumes Command of the Brigade.	S.F.
27..2..16.	Brigadier-General L.R.Carleton, D.S.O. and Captain C.O.Langley, Staff Captain, proceeded overseas on duty.	S.F.
29..2..16.	The 59th (N.M.)Division was exercised in a practice of the Entrainment Scheme, Table "B".	S.F.

L.R. Carleton
B. Genl.
Comdg. 176 th Infantry Bde.

www.ingramcontent.com/pod-product-compliance
Lightning Source LLC
Chambersburg PA
CBHW081515160426
43193CB00014B/2701